Basics of Stock Market

Hardyal Dhairya Vashist

If you purchase this book without a cover, or purchase a PDF, jpg, or tiff copy of this book, it is likely stolen property or a counterfeit. In that case, neither the authors, the publisher, nor any of their employees or agents has received any payment for the copy. Furthermore, counterfeiting is a known avenue of financial support for organised crime and terrorist groups. We urge you to please not purchase any such copy and to report any instance of someone selling such copies to us at dhairyavashist3@gmail.com

Copyright © 2023 by Hardyal Dhairya Vashist

All rights are reserved.

Dedication

This book is dedicated to all those who want to learn the stock market from basics who don't do anything and want to start from scratch.

Preface

I am writing this book because I was very good in academics from the very beginning and I also have interest in finance. But at that time I didn't have any source through which I could understand the Stock Market but I now think that there are many people or children who want to learn about finances and the Stock Market but they don't have any source through which they can do this. For reading this book your age doesn't matter. I tried to tell in a way through which if a 5th grade student will read this then he will also understand this.

Introduction

Before you understand all the things firstly you have to understand why we should do investment. Why don't you keep your money in your home in your locker? Because that can be more safe while you put your money in investments because there can be frauds or scams. But the one reason why we do this is inflation. What is Inflation? You can understand Inflation by this example. Suppose you go to the market today and you buy a chocolate or $1. Can you go to the shop next year and buy that same chocolate in the same pack for $1? You say no. Because you know that the cost of things increases every year. The thing that you can buy, it is possible that in the next year you will become unable. Now some people will say that I have been buying that chocolate for many years for the same price and in the same pack. Then their will be two chances that first chance can be the company reduced the amount.

of that thing or or they started using low quality material to make it. Now I think you can understand what inflation is. And why we don't keep money at our home and why we do investments. Every year inflation increases by average of 6% means if you want to remain your money same or you want that your money value shouldn't decrease. You can understand with this example that the price of properties is increased by how many times. That's called inflation. And that's why you should do investments.

Why should you invest in the stock market?

Some investment ways:

Savings Account

FD/RD

Real Estate

Crypto Currency

Savings Account

In this type of investment you only put your money in the bank in your bank account. From this you get interest of 3-6%. Banks invest your money to give you interest back. I suggest you never put money in your bank till you know that you need less than in 7 days because after this you can make FD of 7 days if you want to play safe. And if you are in your 60s or 70s.

Let's compare it with inflation and all the other things. This can be the worst investment because it is clear that you never beat inflation. This means that you beat inflation sometimes. But not every time. And if you don't beat inflation then the value of your money will decrease.

FD/RD

I have written that FD and RD people think that they are the same but they are not the same. In FD when you have a big amount of money and you make FD (Fixed deposit) in your bank and you get a 6-8% interest on your money after a period of time. Let's understand how it actually works. Banks invest your money and earn money and give you interest. Similar thing for RD but in RD you don't need to give a whole amount of money at a time you have to give money like you give in EMIs.

FD/RD can be your best option if you want to play safe and you are in your 60s or 70s but if you are in your 20s or 30s then I don't suggest you invest all your money in FD.
Let's compare it with inflation and Stock market. As I told you in the beginning, inflation increases by an average percentage of 6%. And FD will give you interest between 6-8% which means it can beat inflation but not every time. If you want money before the maturity period of your FD then you have to pay fines and also your interest rate also decreases means if the interest rate goes less than 6% then you become unable to beat inflation. But think if you meet the inflation. Then you can become sad because you have made an investment so that it can give you money back. But It doesn't.

Real Estate

In this type of investment you buy properties and sell after a period of time. In Real Estate you buy a property and sell that property after some time. During this you can also earn rental income, but there is a problem with it. The problem is you need a lump sum amount of money to buy a property. Real Estate can give you returns between 10%-11% which means it beats inflation, but as I told you the problem. This problem can be solved by REIT(Real Estate Investment Trust) but that doesn't give you rental income.

Crypto Currency

In this you buy something which is coding only what you are buying and if any scam happens to you, in most countries there is no rule for scams of CryptoCurrency. Firstly we have to understand how Crypto Currency price increases or decreases. Suppose a person makes his crypto currency and lists on a crypto exchange and he makes marketing and some people buy it and he increases its price by his choice. Choice means whenever he wants to increase price then he can increase and if he wants to reduce price then he can anytime. Means nothing will affect the price of crypto except the person who made it.

Due to which more people are attracted and they invest in cryptocurrency due to which the person who made that will get more money and he can do anything with that. You can get a profit of 100%-250% or more. This will attract you to invest. You can get a loss 100%. Yes you read and write. That's why many people are only attracted due to that profit but they didn't see the harsh truth of loss and they face loss. I never suggest you invest money in this because you don't know when your money will increase and decrease.

Let's compare it with inflation and other things. As I told you that inflation increases by 6% every year and it can give you 100-250% means it is clear that will beat inflation. But if its value reduces and if any scam happens to you, it means the crypto in which you have invested you get nothing. Then this can be more dangerous than the Savings Account.

Conclusion is it is completely gambling means that it only works on your luck.

Commodities

In this type of investment you buy commodities like gold in the form of jewellery or in the form of digital gold and you keep it for long because the value of gold increases every year due to which you can earn profit by selling them. There are mainly two problems in commodity investing:

- Theft
  There is always a fear of theft for gold because it is a very precious metal.
- Purity
  If you don't have your known jeweller then there is fear that the gold you bought is pure or not.

You can also buy commodities like platinum, silver etc. Commodities give returns between 10%-12% which means it can beat inflation of 6%. But there are some risks in it that I told you.

I have compared all the investment types that maximum people use. There are also many investment types but they are not rather popular and very few people use those to invest your money. Now, you know which investment gives you how much return, now I think that you will be interested in understanding stock because the stock market gives you an average return of 15% which is higher than all of the above except crypto and crypto is also very risky that's why we don't consider it and also many people don't use it as a investment.

What is the Stock Market?

Stock Market is also known as Share Market. This is the place where buying and selling of stocks happen. You can understand the Stock Market by this example. Think that you have a company which makes mobile, so where you go to sell your mobile so that you can find the perfect customer. You will obviously answer, "I will go to the electronics market". Think of it if you have a hotel of 100 rooms. So, where you will go to find customers. You will obviously answer, "I will go to tour and travel websites to show my hotel there so that I can get customers". Think that if you are a farmer and you grow rice and wheat, where do you go? You will obviously answer, "I will go to the market of government middlemen or to the companies who buy it".

From upper examples you know that you have a specified place to sell your thing or to buy something. This is similar for Share or Stock Market. The place where sellers sell their stocks and buyers buy stocks.

Is it gambling?
The answer is yes and no. What this means, there are two types of people who invest in the stock market. First one who first understands the complete stock market and selects their investment company after checking that company's performance, balance sheet, its expenses, its income etc. But the other people didn't see anything, they heard from their friend that he earned money from this stock so I also invested in that stock and I will also earn money or my stock value will increase. Means they are investing in their luck, means if he loses then it's his luck and if he makes profit then it's his luck. Such people can earn money one time but not every time. For the first type of people the stock market is not gambling but for the second type of people the stock market is gambling.

What is the Stock Exchange?
The place where exactly the buying or selling of shares happens is known as the stock exchange. These stock exchanges are located in big cities. Stock exchanges can be one or two or more like the U.S has two Stock exchanges: the New York Stock Exchange (NYSE) and the National Association of Securities Dealers Automated Quotation System (Nasdaq). Similarly India has two stock exchanges NSE(National Stock Exchange) and BSE (Bombay Stock Exchange) and these both are located in Mumbai City of India. These stock exchanges are regulated by a government regulatory body. Like in India stock exchanges are regulated by SEBI (Security and Exchange Board of India).

Does buying and selling take place physically?
The answer is no today. But many years ago it took place physically but nowadays you can buy and sell stocks from your mobile, tablet, laptop or from your computer. But in past means, past means not many centuries ago it means sown decades the buying or selling was taken place physically but after the coming of Internet all the things became online due to which buying and selling can be taken place within seconds.

Can people from other countries buy stocks of any other country?

The answer is Yes. People from other countries can buy shares of any other country's company. There are two types through which a person buys stocks of companies in other countries:

- FDI (Foreign Direct Investment)
  This is done by big companies who are also doing their business and they buy stocks directly from that company. And if a company gets a loss then that company also has to face loss and they also can't sell their shares.

- FII (Foreign Institutional Investors)
  This is done by investors who buy stocks from stock exchanges because they don't have billions of dollars so that they can buy directly from the companies. And due to this they also have a benefit that they can sell their shares at any time whenever they want, and due to which they don't have to face such a big loss.

What are shares?

Suppose you are the owner of a company which manufactures pencils and you want money, then you give ownership or partnership with other people. Suppose your company valuation is $10,000 and you launch 10,000 shares which means 1 share value is $1. Now a question arises in your mind, how many shares can be launched by a company. The answer is it depends on the company. If they want that we will launch 100,000 then it's their choice which means that there are no limits on the number of shares that company is launching. Share remains in the market that was launched during the time of IPO, after launching its IPO, the company doesn't launch its more shares.

What are Penny Stocks?

You have seen many stocks that are under the value of $5 and these stocks are known as penny stocks in America, not in every country, for different countries this value is different. Means you can say that if you are living in any country, the small denomination of your currency. All countries don't fix that value. For ex if you are in India then Penny stocks for you can be those stocks less than 1 rupee

Who are Stock Brokers?

You can't buy or sell stocks directly from stock exchanges. If you want to do this then you have to use a middleman who works to make a connection between you and stock exchanges. So that you can buy or sell stocks without any problem. Now a question will arise in your mind: do they do this for free? The answer is no. They charge a fee from investors known as brokerage. This fee varies from broker to broker. And that middle man is known as a broker. This middle man can be an app, can be a website or can be a man. But you should choose a trusted Stock Broker.

What is Market Order?

Suppose you have checked all the things about a stock and now you have made up your mind that I will buy this stock. So simply what you do you will place order to buy that so the stock will be purchased on that time stock price. And this is the same for selling: suppose you have to sell a stock then you will place an order to sell your stocks, so you I'll receive money on that time stock price. Suppose if the current price of a stock is $10 then it will be purchased for $10 and if you want to sell a stock and if its current value is $15 then you will get $15 in your trading account.

What is a Limiting Order?

Suppose you want to buy a stock and you saw that at this time the price of stock is high but you want to buy it for a low price. So, what will you do? You will say that I will wait till when the price of stock decreases but you don't because the broker you are using will provide you an option of limiting order. Let's understand it with an example: suppose now the current price of a stock is $20 and you want that I will buy it at $15. So what you will do. You will place a limiting order from your trading account means whenever this price will be reached the stock will be purchased for you. This is similar to selling if you want to sell a stock and now its current price is $10 and you want to sell it at $25 then you will place a limiting order for selling a stock so that the stocks will be purchased or sold when that price is reached.

What is a Demat Account?

I ask you a question. Do you know what a bank account does? You will obviously answer, "The place where you can store your money without any risk of theft". Means the place where you can store your money. Now after this I will ask you a question again where do you store your stocks and other electronic bought assets. The answer is Demat Account. The place where you can store your electronic bought assets. These can be stocks, digital gold etc. And if you want to invest money in the Stock Market then firstly you should have a Demat Account. There are many free ways through which you can open a demat account and after opening a demat account, you will also get an account number as you get your bank account number.

What is a Trading Account?

Now I think that you know what a Demat account is. But now you will ask me a question why there is a Trading Account. Demat account is used to store your electronic format assets but Trading Account is used to buy stocks. Means if you want to buy any stock then firstly you have to transfer money in your trading account from a Bank Account and then you can buy it. And if you sell any stock then the money you will get in your Trading Account which you can transfer to your bank account or use it to buy more stocks. Means if you want to buy or sell any stock you have to place an order from your trading account.

What are Indices?

If you want to see the average of any stock exchange, what would you do? Means if you see if the stock exchange goes up or down then you will see Indices. These are like averages of any stock exchange because in this we only have the country's top most companies. Means we can say that if these Indices are going up then this means stock exchange is performing better or if Indices are going down then this means stock exchange is not performing better. But sometimes this can be completely opposite because companies in these Indices are changed by these stock exchanges and sometimes these Indices go down but some companies perform so much better. Because every stock exchange has thousands of companies listed. So, no one can say that all the companies are going up or going down. But from this we can get average. And in this all types of companies are involved like finance, cement, electronics and some others. These Indices are also named like for New York Stock Exchange we consider Dow Jones Industrial for BSE (Bombay Stock Exchange) in India Sensex is considered which is average of top 30 most performing companies. And for NSE (National Stock Exchange) in India which is an average of top 50 most performing companies.

What is holding time?
As you can understand from its name. Means this the time for which you buy stock and don't sell for a period of time. Like if you buy a stock and hold it for 1 year then your stock holding time is 1 year because you haven't sold it. This holding time can be as minimum as you can think. And as maximum as you can think. Like you ask me if I buy a stock for some seconds and sell it for some seconds then it will be known as holding time.

What is Liquidity?

Suppose you have bought some stocks and you want to sell them but you don't get anyone who can buy your stock or there are very small number of people who are ready to buy it then the liquidity of that stock will be very low and if you want to sell a stock and many people are ready to buy it then this means that stock liquidity is high. This can also be for buying means if you want to buy any stock and there are no sellers then that stock liquidity is low and if you want to buy a stock and there are many sellers then this means that stock liquidity is high. Means how easy you can buy or sell a stock is called its liquidity. If you can easily buy or sell any stock then it's liquidity is high and if you have to struggle to buy or sell a stock then it's liquidity is low.

What is Volatility?

Suppose you have seen a stock now who's price is very low but you saw it after some time or some hours and now its price has become very high. This will be the same if you saw a stock and its price is very high but after some time its price becomes low then its volatility is high. And if the price of a stock doesn't change very fast means it doesn't go up fastly or come down fastly then its volatility is low. You can understand it with this example now you have seen price of a stock is $10 but after some time you saw that it's price become $15 then it's volatility is very high and if it's price was $20 but after some time its price become $10 then volatility is high and if its price was $20 then it's value become $19.59 then volatility is very low.

What is Market Capitalisation?

As you can understand from the name market and capitalisation means the value of all shares present in the market of a company is known as market capitalisation of a company. Means from this we can understand how good a company is performing but this can become opposite. Because sometimes stock values are increased or decreased by pump and dump. We can understand this with this example for if the price of a share of a company is $100 and the total number of shares present in the market is 1,000,000 then the market capitalization of that company will be $100,000,000 or 100 million dollars. The formula to find market capitalisation of a company is. Market Capitalisation= Current price of share*Total number of shares in the market.

What are Outstanding shares?

Suppose a company had made themselves public and they released their shares but not all the released shares are not purchased or all the shares are purchased by the investors. Means all shares that are purchased by investors are called outstanding shares. The formula to find it is. Outstanding Shares= Total number of shares released-Total number of shares purchased by investors or issued for investors. Sometimes company officials purchase their shares so that's why the other formulae can be. Outstanding shares= Number of issued shares-number of shares held in company treasury.

What are Large Cap Companies, Mid Cap Companies and Small cap companies ?

Cap means capitalisation means how much capitalisation a company has and according to their capitalisation companies are divided into three types:

- Large Cap Companies
- Mid Cap Companies
- Small Cap Companies

Large Cap Companies:
Those companies which have capitalization of more than 10 billion dollars are called Large Cap Companies.

Mid Cap Companies:
Those companies which have capitalization between 2 billion and 10 billion dollars.

Small Cap Companies:
Those companies which have capitalization less than 2 billion dollars.

What is an IPO?

You have heard in ads or from people that this company is launching their IPO or this company is launching their IPO. Suppose there is a person named Z. He already has two or three partners or he is a single owner but now his company has become very big. And now he wants to list his company on a Stock Exchange or he wants to release his shares because he wants money. So, whenever he launches his shares for the first time, this first time launching of shares is known as IPO (Initial Public Offering). And retail investors like you can buy their stocks.

What is Diversification?
As you can understand from the name diverse. Means you invest by diversifying.You can get confused. Let's understand this with an example. Suppose you are an investor who invests in a pharma industry, which means you invest in a medicine related company and you make your whole investment in a single industry. But due to this you can face loss because if the pharma industry crashes or goes down then you have to face loss means there is a very high risk of loss. Whereas if you invest in many industries like electronics, pharma, finance etc. Then there will be a very low chance that you face loss because if any industry goes down then your not whole investment will give you loss but you can get even more profit because when some industries crash and some industries flourish that's why you should diversify because it decreases the chance of loss.

What are Blue Chip Companies?

You have heard from many people that as a beginner you should invest in bluechip because these are those reputed companies who are working for many years or decades and investors show so much interest in investing in these types of companies. So, you should invest because there will be a very low chance in the long term that you will face loss. So, you should start your investing from these blue chip companies.

What is Stock Split?

You have heard that a company has a stock split but what does this mean? Let's understand, in this case companies split the number of stocks into multiple stocks. Let's understand this with the example of suppose you have a denomination of $100 and you will split it into 10 denominations of $10. But now the value of your all 10 denominations of $10 remains the same but the value decreases according to the ratio of split. Let's understand with stocks, if a company announces a 2 for 1 stock split then each share will be divided into 2 shares meaning if you have 100 shares then after the split you will get 200 shares. And due to this the price of a share also decreased to half.

What are Share Market animals?

There are ten animals of share market:
- Bull
- Bear
- Sheep
- Turtle
- Snail
- Chicken
- Ship
- Rabbit
- Shark
- Whale

Let's understand all this.

Bull

Imagine that a bull is running so his head always remains down and his horn remains ahead and whenever it pushes anyone he/she will go up not down. Means the person who can grow the Indices. Now you will say how he/she will increase the Indices, he will invest money and the market will go up, they buy stocks at any price they get due to which the stock market will go up. Or we can say that the person who increases the price of stock. And as you know the market depends on demand and supply. The bull increases the demand but supply doesn't increase due to which price increases. And the big bulls are those who can increase the price of a stock as much as they want.

Bear

Whenever you see a bear he always throws a person down, not up means the person who will decrease the price of a stock. This also depends on the demand and supply means if supply will increase and demand remains the same then the price will decrease. Suppose if price a person has so much stocks and he sell all his stocks due to which the price decrease and if there is rumour that price will decrease then all the people will sell their stocks and the person who spread this rumour he buy stock from all those people who want to sell due that rumour. And due to this the price will decrease firstly but when that person will buy all the stocks the price will increase and he will sell his stock and earn profits.

Turtle

Those who buy a stock and sell it for a period of time. Those people who use mutual funds to invest in stocks also come in the category of turtles. This time period is very large like years or decades. But for these types of things there is very low risk because they invest for a long time. You also fall in the category of turtle if you are invested for long periods or you play safe.

Snail

Whenever you imagine a snail you imagine that an animal mostly lives under the surface. And never cared what others are doing or we can say that these are those people who use traditional ways to invest. Means they will prefer FDs or bank deposits. If you said to them that you can do this they can't and they also never use their own mind. To make decisions about what is happening for decades due to which they have to face problems.

Chicken

Chicken are those investors who always remain scared because whenever you see a chicken if any problem comes to it like heavy winds etc. Then they come out of their poultry and stay out and they do this when they are scared, if there is a very short problem, in that problem also they will remain scared. And these of investors who take decisions in feelings, if anyone said to them that market is going down then they will sell their all stocks without caring that Indices is only a average of some companies and there are thousands of companies listed on a stock exchange they don't check their purchased company share but the only thing they do they will sell their shares because they think that there all money will be destroyed.

Sheep
Whenever you imagine a sheep you imagine that they always live in big groups. They never take decisions without the permission of their handler. Permission means not to stand or sit but permission they never go anywhere with their mind or we can say sheep don't have their own mind. They always ask others if I can invest in this stock, is it good for me. And they always invest in the same stock whether the company is performing or not.

Pig
Pig is considered the worst among all animals because you can imagine what a pig's reputation is. This is similar to that person who is considered a pig. The person who borrows money from others and invests money but never gets satisfied with the returns is known as pig. The pig is also considered as greedy because he never satisfies from the returns. Pig is that person who takes so much risk so much means so much due to which he also has to face loss sometimes. He/she never invests to gain knowledge but they invest due only for returns.

Wolf

Wolves are the most greedy and powerful animals. Because they earn so much money through illegal ways. Means they will do insider trading due to which or they get news of inside the company what company is going to do on the next day. Means if they get news that a company is going to release their stocks at a low price then they sell all their stocks and earn money. But the ways Wolf uses are illegal due to which governments take action on them and they get punished. But many people are scammed by these Wolves.

Ostrich

As you know, it has a very long neck and it never flies. But whenever a tornado comes he closes his eyes and hides his neck inside the soil and he thinks that tornado will not harm it. But it harms its upper body. These types of people make decisions for their portfolio like a joke, meaning they don't care what is actually happening in the market, they do what they want or if anyone tells them to do this then they will do that, they don't care if they have to face loss in future.

Rabbit

As you know, the characteristics of a rabbit that he jumps faster and faster means the person who buys and sells stock for a very short period of time or for a day. You can understand this with this example. If a person buys a stock in the morning and sells it in the evening then we will say that he is Rabbit. Rabbit's earn or lose money so fast. Means we can say that those people who do trading for a very short period of time. This time can be a week or a day or an hour.

Shark

Imagine a shark, a horrible animal that eats other fishes and a dangerous animal who can even eat humans as you see in movies. We can say that this is similar to the stock market, these are big players. Let's understand this with an example. Suppose an IPO is coming and the shark told some small fishes that give me your money you will get this profit and that profit. And these small fishes also give their money. Small fishes are those middle class or poor people who don't have such knowledge of the stock market. The shark invests money of all those people in the stock due to which it goes up and people think that, yes our money is growing when the scam fails the stock of that company comes down so fast.

What is Insider Trading?

Suppose if anyone has information inside a company means he has the information, that after sometime this company is going to launch its IPO but no one knows about this in the market. And he buys some equity before the launching of the IPO at a lower price than the value at which the IPO is coming. Now, a question will arise in your mind? Why do they do this? They do this because they think I get this at a low price and I will sell it at a higher price through which I can earn profit. But it's illegal, but it destroys the integrity of the stock market.

What is Equity?

Let's understand it by an example: suppose a person named Y owns a company and his company valuation is $100,000. And he wants money to expand his business. So, he finds a partner who can do partnership so that he can get money to expand. The partner gives him $10000. This means the partner had given Y 10% of Y company's valuation. This means Y has to give 10% of ownership to his partner. And this 10% ownership is known as equity. This can be more percentage as it is a number game.

Why do companies launch their shares?

Let's understand this with an example. Think that you have a company in which you make chocolates. You make chocolate in one factory which you have but you want to expand your business. So, what you will do is you have three options. First, you take out a loan from the bank. Second is you borrow money from your friend or relative. Third is you give ownership to any person due to which he will give you money. It depends on the company. Suppose if a company's valuation is $100,000. Companies choose the third option to get money. Now one more question will arise in your mind. What these companies do with this money. This answer is simple: if any company gives ownership then this means they don't have money in cash. That's why they are giving and after they get money, suppose the company was of chocolates which has 1 factory now they can make one more factory to increase their production.

What is the Stock Market Crash?

There are many companies listed on a stock exchange and the maximum companies lose the price of their stock by ten percent is a known market crash. Means that is a situation that can't be predicted by anyone. Means it is similar to earthquakes that you can't predict like cyclones or weather. It is unpredictable. You can understand it by this example: suppose you bought a share yesterday for $100 and its price becomes $20 today. Like you, many people also bought that share and thousands of people bought that. Suppose a thousand people bought that then the total value will be $100,000 and today's price will become $20,000. Nor can you clearly see the loss of $80,000. And this is only for one company, suppose the maximum of companies share price decreases.

Reasons of Stock Market Crash

There are mainly seven reasons of stock market crash:

- **Territory activities**
- **War**
- **Change of government**
- **Scam**
- **Bubble Burst**
- **Pandemic**
- **Trade Wars**

Terrorist Activities

Suppose if an alert is released by the government that terrorist activity can happen, what people will do is they will take out their money from companies because they think that anything can happen, and they do this because of their fear. Many international investors also take their money from the market. Due to which FDI decreases. This is also because if there is alert, then tourists don't visit that country for some days due to which that country's GDP (Gross Domestic Product) also gets affected due to which market crashes and FDI doesn't come in that country for some days.

War
Due to wars, the market crashes due to many reasons. One of the major reasons why stock market crashes is because the tourism sector gets affected and tourists will not visit that country due to which that country's tourism sector gets affected. And many companies are directly related to the tourism sector. Second reason is sanctions. In a war many countries apply sanctions on one another. Due to which foreign investors don't invest in that country and that country's FDI (Foreign Direct Investment) will be stopped. And if demand decreases then automatically price decreases.

Change of government

There are mainly two types of parties in every country leftist and rightists. Leftist are those people who support having power in the hands of every individual, which means they think that power should not be in the hand of one person. Whereas Rightist are completely opposite to Leftist. They support that power should be in the hand of one person not in the hand of a group of people. Due to Leftist and Rightist wing, sometimes the government makes decisions according to their wing. Or sometimes if one party wants to make friends with a country and other don't die to which FDI got affected.

Scam

There are many scams in the stock market that get exposed. But there are some people who see these scams as a type of golden opportunity because if any scam get exposed people will sell their stocks due to which price will decrease so much and those smart people will buy stocks at low price and sell them at high prices when everything becomes normal because you have to understand that if stock market crashes it heals by 125%, by 146% these type of increases come in market after the market crash.

Bubble Burst

Bubble worst is the worst thing because due to this many people get affected. You can understand this by an example. Suppose if there is a company which shows that they are earning a profit of 30% but in reality they are only earning 2% or 3% then when this bubble bursts people withdraw their money from the market. And suppose if there is a company which shows we are in profit but they get exposed when people get to know that, that company is in loss. Then again people will withdraw their money from the market. Due to which the market crashed.

Pandemic

Suppose if any disease comes and it changes into pandemic then what will happen. I think you have seen in the covid period, how the country's economies were going in minus. And again the same tourism sector got affected, FDI will not reach that country and that country's people also don't invest due to which price will come down because demand decreases and if demand decreases then price automatically decreases. And you noticed a thing that pharmaceutical companies earned so much profits in those days. And those online companies who sell their product in electronic format also gain profit.

Trade War

Suppose if the relations between two countries are not good and they apply sanctions on one another and they said to their friends you should apply sanctions on that country. So, what will happen is people will not travel in those which are sanctioned by their country and Investors will not invest in those countries on which sanctions are applied by their country. And this not only harms those two countries but all the countries that trade with those countries will get affected because due to sanctions prices will increase and if price will increase then inflation will increase and if inflation increases then people become unable to invest money and again market get affected.

Let's understand an example of the worst market crash due to which the whole world was affected. This is known as the crisis of 2008 which happened because a bank named as Lehman brothers failed. Let's understand this story. As you all know about the attack of 9/11 which happened on the World Trade Centre in America. This story starts from there. Between 2001 and 2004 people were so much feared due to which they didn't invest money because people were thinking that anyone would attack America. And due to this Federal Reserve Bank of America decreased interest rates on housing loans from 6% to directly between 1.5% to 1.75%. FRBA (Federal Reserve Bank of America) so that people can take money and spend it in the market, so that the economy of America can grow.

Due to this, those people who don't have money also take loans from the banks. And banks always give you money on the behalf of collateral, which means the asset that the bank can sell if you don't pay money. So, people started buying properties after taking a loan from the bank and giving the bank their property documents as a collateral. Due to that real estate market getting a huge boom and those properties which can be bought for $100,000 after this, their price has become $300,000 means there is a sudden increase of 300%. This is only for example. Means banks give the loan for $300,000 valuation but the actual price was $100,000. And similar to other banks there was a bank named as Lehman Brothers. It was so old that it was founded in 1850 means it's a 173 year old bank (according to 2023). It was the 4th biggest bank of America at that time.

Lehman Brothers bank has a mortgage of 600 billion dollars meaning they have the documents of properties whose value is 600 billion dollars and they had given that money to those people who gave their property documents. For every bank there are two types of customer:

- Prime Customer
  These customers are those customers on which banks have so much trust means they can give loans back in any situation and they also have a good record with the bank.
- Subprime Customers
  These are those customers who will not give loan back if any problem happens with them and banks don't have any record of those customers before giving loans.

In that time subprime customers were taking so many loans from banks and especially from Lehman Brothers bank. And after a period of time a time will come when they want their money back means those depositors who deposited their money in the bank. But from where does banks get money, from their depositors. But when depositors want their money the bank has to pay but Lehman Brothers bank doesn't have money, so what do they do? They went to a third party which was a bank and said to them, "Take these 100 billion dollars worth of property documents and give us 100 billion dollars. So, that third party asked what benefit I would get from this. Then Lehman Brothers bank said "you will get the interest rate that we are getting and an extra 1% interest rate". So, that third party said, "Ok".

And Lehman Brothers bank gave those property papers to that third party as a CDO (Collateral Debt Obligation). But when that third party gets to know that those people who take out a loan from Lehman Brothers bank are poor people, it means they have to get a loss if they don't pay. So, what Lehman Brothers bank did was they said to a third party, "That we will also change this CDO in insurance, so that if anything happens then you can claim insurance". And that insurance company was AIG (American International Group). So, give insurance to that 100 billion dollars CDO, meaning if Lehman Brothers didn't give money to that party then AIG will give. Lehman brothers had to pay some money that has to be paid by anyone if you take insurance.

As we saw that all the things happened due to decrease in interest rates. But when interest rates decrease inflation increases. FRBA has to control this inflation so they changed the interest rates from between 1.5%-1.75% directly to 6%. Means those people who took a loan at 1.5%-1.75%, now they have to pay a loan at 6%. So, Lehman Brothers asked for their money back and people said that we don't have money and you can sell our properties to get money. So, Lehman Brothers started bidding the properties but when people got to know about this. So, they thought, why do we buy it at such a high cost? Lehman Brothers bank needed money and they would sell it at any cost. And those properties which were of $300,000 but no one was ready to buy it at $100,000.

And that third party gets to know about this that at which they have given money for properties are not real. But they were tension free because they have insurance done by AIG. So, they asked AIG to give them money, so AIG said, "We are sorry, we don't have money, we do this because Lehman Brothers bank was so reputed and we were thinking this will never happen, and we do this to earn money". And this was the day of 15 September 2008. And then Lehman Brothers bank printed a letter and gave it to the government that we are now bankrupt and we are unable to give money. And this AIG has given insurance to many companies, so the American government provided money to AIG and purchased 80% shares so that all those companies also don't become bankrupt. And due to this the American stock market fell by 57% in one day.

What is Buyback?

Suppose a company launched their IPO at a price of $2,000 but now the price of their share became $500 and they started buying it from those investors. You can understand it by this example. Suppose you bought a phone at $2,000 due to its features but after buying it you get to know that the phone you bought has the same features which your old phone has. So, what you will do you try to sell it to other person, suppose you sold it at a price of $1,900 and the person who bought from you also sold it to the other person and this continues, after some time that phone price become $500 and only you were not doing this many people were doing this. But when the company gets to know about it, their $2,000 is selling at $500. So, what about that company? That company started buying their phone from the people. And due to which the price of their mobile phone increased. This is the same for stock, the price of that company stock also increases.

What is Share Market balancing?

Suppose if so much Foreign investment is withdrawn by foreign investors but at that time also how the market becomes stable. For this firstly we have two understand two terms:

- Primary Market

  When a company launches its IPO and people buy shares directly from the company, this market where buying and selling takes place directly from the company is known as Primary Market.

- Secondary Market

  Companies launch their IPO only one time, so how can you buy shares after the launching of an IPO, if all shares were sold at the launching of the IPO. You buy shares from investors like you want to sell their shares, this market where buying and selling do not take place between the company but between the two investors is known as a secondary market.

Because at the same time other people also buy stocks, and this happens in India most of the time due to which many experts say,"We should learn from Indians how they balance their stock market when Foreign Investors withdraw money". And you know that whenever the price of a share goes down people will buy it due to which its price goes up and that's the reason why after crashes the stock market goes up two times or more of the loss that happened in the stock market.

What is Stop Loss?

Suppose you have bought a share and you think that this share can go down or suppose there are no chances that this stock can down but you don't want to take risk, so what you will do, you will apply stop loss on that stock means if that stock reaches that value on which you have applied stop loss then stock will be automatically sold after reaching that price. Now you ask me who will sell this. The answer is Broker. Let's understand this with an example: suppose you bought a share of $10 and you want that if the price reaches $9 then you can gain loss but you think that if this share reaches the price of $9 and 50 cents then it will sell automatically, so apply stop loss at 9 dollar and 50 cents.

What is Pump and Dump?

Suppose there is a person who bought shares of a company in the past but now he wants to sell his shares but now the price of shares is very low, so what he will do, he will give ransom to a stock market operator and say to him that you have to increase this stock price. That operator will start buying and selling shares between two accounts . Not only that operator, many people are involved in it. Due to which price of a share will increase 5% to 10%. And these operators will send messages to people that these famous investors or businessmen have invested money in this. But these investors hadn't invested which means these messages are fake. Suppose if they sent messages to 1 million people and if only ten thousand people trust them and buy that share then this will also be a big game for them.

Some investors don't get influenced by this, so what these operators do. They will give money to those experts who come on TV shows related to the stock market and these experts say to people that you should buy these shares. Some people are influenced by this. But some people are smart and they don't do this. So, what these operators do is that they publish news in the newspapers and media houses that this company team has taken strict decisions due to which it is growing. And due to all this the price of stock increases by so much percent. And now the operator will say to that person who gives him money that you can do anything. Now that person will start selling his shares and he will not sell his shares consecutively; he will sell in a period of time, so that the market doesn't become aware that this is pump and dump.

And after some time the price of that stock will reach its actual value on which it was started pumping. Pumping means the process in which the price of a stock is increased in some ways. And this is illegal. Dumping means the automatic process that happens when that person who wants to sell his stocks starts selling his stocks. Some people get stuck in it due to which they have to face a high and they tell the market that don't invest in it, you will lose your money. And if you noticed a thing that all the people invested only due to greed and without checking about that company.

What is SIP?

SIP (Systematic Investment Plan), through its name you will think that it's so complicated but it is not. You have heard that many people become millionaires or billionaires. But they don't become when they invest $100 and it becomes $150. They come through SIP. In SIP you invest some amount every month, that amount can be anything, meaning you can even start with $10. Or you can invest $100,000 per month. That's your choice, your money becomes such a big amount after years through compounding. Let's understand it with an example. Suppose you have started a SIP of $100 every month for 10 years at an expected return rate of 12%, the total amount you invested is $12,000 and it becomes $23,234 which is almost double. Suppose if you have started a SIP of $100 and you duck it, and almost 100 years, then you have invested $120,000 and it will become $1,548,699,224. What is this number? You only invested thousands of dollars and it became billions.

Earning through Dividend

Let's understand this with an example that a company is owned by a person named as A. He will release shares and his company valuation is $10,000 and he launches 10,000 shares (now we are considering that he will launch complete ownership to the market) which means his one share value is $1, so let's think if his company get's a profit of $1,000 then on every 1 share 1 cent will be given. From this we can understand dividends are a very large amount of money but companies launch these. Companies can give dividends monthly, quarterly or annually. Generally companies give dividends quarterly and annually.

There are mainly 5 types of dividends:
- Cash dividend
- Property dividend
- Scrip dividend
- Liquidating dividend
- Stock Dividend

Cash dividend:

In this type of dividend companies will give you dividends in the form of money.

There are two types of cash dividends:
- Interim dividend
- Final dividend

Interim dividend:

It is given by the company in 3 months, which means quarterly.

Final dividend:

It is given by the company annually.

Property dividend:
In this type of dividend company will give you money in the form of a property.

Scrip dividend:
In this type of dividend company gives you a guarantee that we will give your dividends in future.

Liquidating dividend:
In this type of dividend company will give you guarantee that when the company will dissolve your dividend will be given to you on the basis of that day's company valuation.

Stock dividend:
In this type of dividend company will say to you that we will give more shares to you on the value of your dividend.

Dividend percentage is always calculated on the face value of a share (price of share when it was launched or price when IPO was launched).

What is a Bonus Issue?

Whenever companies want to reward their investors, they issue bonuses for their investors in the form of shares when the company doesn't have money. If companies have money then why don't they issue dividends for their shareholders? Due to this the number of shares in the market of a company increases due to which liquidity also increases. Let's understand it with an example: if a company announces a 5 for 1 bonus issue then if you already have 100 shares of that company then you will get 500 shares for free and your total number of shares will become 600.

What is SWP?

Suppose you have some money now which you want to invest but it's a big amount, then there are many options in which you can invest but if you want that it also works as a pension so that you can get a regular income from it, so in that situation you can use SWP (Systematic Withdrawal Plan). This is opposite of SIP because you invest a certain amount every month and you get a big amount after some years but in SWP you invest a big amount and you get it every month. And on this you will also get interest.

In this also you give your money to a mutual fund. Let's understand how it actually works? Suppose you have invested $100,000. And one unit value is $10 (Unit is similar to stocks like you buy stocks you buy units not directly but mutual fund buys it on your behalf) then you will get 10,000 units but value of unit go up and down because stock market go up and down. Means if you started a FPO of $100 and today 1 unit price is $10 then your 10 units will be sold but if today price of 1 unit is $20 then 5 units will be sold. Experts think that you should make 4% of SWP every year of your total invested amount because your SWP will never end.

What is a Co-location scam?

As I told you that stock exchanges are present at a fixed place and if you want to buy stock then you have to buy it from your demat account. Let's understand this with the example of the New York Stock Exchange. Suppose you live in Los Angeles and you want to buy a stock from NYSE (New York Stock Exchange) and as you know information takes time to travel means if now there is a stock available of $1 but that's not its actual value because it remains between $2-$3 and now you place order but when you place an order your order doesn't take place because anyone bought it before you. Now suppose anyone is sitting on a side of all those supercomputers in the stock exchange who are managing all the trading and you get to know about before anyone then you can easily earn profits, because there is a latency (the time difference between the information is made and you get to know about it after some time is called latency) between you and the person who is sitting with that computer then he will place order because in stock market in fractions of seconds billions of trade happens. And due to all this he will get to know about every information before anyone in the world and earns profit and this is illegal.

There are mainly 5 types of ratios:
- Profitability Ratios
- Liquidity Ratios
- Solvency Ratios
- Activity Ratios
- Valuation Ratios

Profitability Ratios

As you can understand it from its name means it is related to profits of a company means how much profits a company is making and what is its position in the market. Means if any company is not earning profits then this means that a problem is going on with that company. Means if a company X is earning profit of 30% and another company named as Z is earning profits of 50% then Z is better than X in terms of profit. Formula to find it is Profit = Income statement-Expenses and Liabilities and formula to calculate profit margin is Net Profit/Sales Value.

Liquidity Ratios

This is the ratio that tells whether any company is able to pay its debt in the short term. It means how comfortable a company is. Let's understand this: suppose there is a company whose debt is so much more than its yearly profits. This means that a company is not able to pay its debt comfortably and there is a company whose debt is so much less or that company doesn't have debt then that company is comfortable to pay its loan back. The formula to find it is Current Ratio = Current Assets/Current Liabilities.

Solvency Ratios

As you know liquidity ratio tells about how a company is comfortable to give its debt in short term and solvency ratio tells us how comfortable a company is to repay its debt. It is also known as Leverage Ratio and Debt Ratio. Means if any company is not comfortable to repay its debt then it is considered good and if any company is comfortable to repay its debt then this means that that company is good in terms of repaying its loan. The formula to find is Debt Ratio = Total Liabilities/Total Assets.

Activity Ratios

This means that a company is managing its assets and liabilities and is trying to gain more assets and lose liabilities as much as they can. If any company is not earning from its assets then this means that those assets which the company is showing are not assets or they are taken by the company on the loan due to which the company loses all its money in repaying the loan. It is also known as efficiency ratios or asset utilisation ratios. The formula to find it is Cost of goods sold/Average Inventory.

Valuation Ratios

It is mainly used for how a company makes investment decisions and what is the right value of the company. And according to the valuation of companies we divide them into three types as I told you. The formula to find it is Earning Per Share = Net Profit/Number of Outstanding Shares.

Conclusion

I think all the basics of stock market are clear and now you can move on to learn the stock market deeply because now you will not find any problem in understanding higher knowledge of picking stocks. There are many things that change in the stock market and if you want to stay updated about all that then you can subscribe to my free newsletter on galyam.substack.com where I always try to increase your financial knowledge.

www.ingramcontent.com/pod-product-compliance
Lightning Source LLC
Chambersburg PA
CBHW050246220526
45465CB00002B/574